for FREDERICK *and* LEE PETERSON

ποῖ λευκὸν ἵππον

ARISTOPHANES

LYSISTRATA

AN ENGLISH VERSION
BY DUDLEY FITTS

FABER AND FABER

3 Queen Square

London

First published in this edition 1960
by Faber and Faber Limited
3 Queen Square London W.C.1
Second revised edition 1965
Reprinted 1967, 1971 and 1974
Printed in Great Britain by
Alden & Mowbray Ltd
at the Alden Press, Oxford
All rights reserved
© 1959, 1962 by Dudley Fitts

ISBN 0 571 07020 5 (Faber Paper Covered Editions)

INTRODUCTORY NOTE

i

Lysistrata was written in 412 B.C., and the evidence points to its production at the Athenian festival of the Lenaia in January 411. It is the last of the three plays that Aristophanes devoted to the subject of the war with Sparta—the others being *The Acharnians* and *Peace*—and it is the bravest of them. Never had the situation of Athens been more nearly desperate. The great military and naval expedition to Sicily, that almost maniacal gesture of *hybris,* had been utterly destroyed at Syracuse in 413; and though there were to be seven more years of confusion and despair before the final collapse at the battle of Aigospotomoi, it was clear to Aristophanes, as it must have been to any thinking man, that the cause was lost. *Lysistrata* was an attempt to stem the rush towards annihilation, to save something from the wreckage before it should be too late to save anything. The attempt failed. Nothing was saved. Yet the comedy remains, a generous and shining affirmation of confidence in the ultimate sanity of mankind; and the topical references and symbolic horseplay that attach it to its time neither lessen its enduring urgency nor reduce the importance of what it has to say to us in our similar predicament.

The play is ribald, by any standards. Partly this was an attempt to make laughter succeed where rage and tears, not to speak of common sense, had failed. Partly, too, it was ritualistic, or semi-ritualistic: the origin of Old Comedy in ancient fertility rites is reflected in the theme of *Lysistrata*; and the pseudo-epithalamion in the *éxodos,* like the true ones that conclude *Birds* and *Peace,* seems to have been enforced to a certain extent by tradition. The outrageous and daring plot, however, owes nothing to tradition. It is shock that counts, the elemental shock of good sense insisted upon to the point of absurdity. For what could be more sensible, more wildly absurd, than that the women on both sides should call a sexual strike to halt a war that no

3

longer had meaning or promised hope? 'On both sides'; for
Aristophanes addresses himself to Sparta as well as to
Athens, and there is no time-wasting talk of international
inspections to guard against secret tests, copulations under-
ground or (as in *Birds*) in the air. No one could possibly
take Lysistrata's proposition seriously; it is a joke, brutally
pure; but the absurd has its own tragic depths, and it may
be that our simplicities offer more hope at the end than
all our complexities and distinctions.

ii

This translation is based upon a version published in
1954, the first of my attempts to put Aristophanes into
English. It was an unequal but generally unsatisfactory
attempt, largely because of the many freedoms I permitted
myself in handling the text, especially the lyric passages.
I have welcomed the opportunity afforded by this collection
to rewrite certain passages and to revise others; but since
my primary intention was, and is, to write an actable and
sayable play, I must warn those who do not know *Lysistrata*
in Greek that this is still a free version, not translation *ad
litteram expressa*. The low-comedy burlesque of Deep South
talk is retained, in spite of the many perfectly lucid ob-
jections by scholars, in the passages involving the delegates
from Sparta; the Athenian Drunkard who turned up, without textual authority, in the earlier version, has also been
kept; and throughout, but especially in the *éxodos*, there
has been a conjectural, though I hope discreet, redistribu-
tion of speeches.

CONTENTS

LYSISTRATA
KALONIKE
MYRRHINE
LAMPITO
CHORUS
COMMISSIONER
KINESIAS
SPARTAN HERALD
SPARTAN AMBASSADOR
A SENTRY

SCENE: *Athens. First, a public square; later, beneath the walls of the Akropolis; later, a courtyard within the Akropolis.*

Until the *éxodos,* the CHORUS is divided into two hemichori: the first, of Old Men; the second, of Old Women. Each of these has its KORYPHAIOS. In the *éxodos,* the hemichori return as Athenians and Spartans.

The supernumeraries include the BABY SON of Kinêsias; STRATYLLIS, a member of the hemichorus of Old Women; various individual speakers, both Spartan and Athenian.

🎭 PROLOGUE

> [*Athens; a public square; early morning;* LYSISTRATA *sola*

LYSISTRATA:
  If someone had invited them to a festival—
  of Bacchos, say; or to Pan's shrine, or to Aphroditê's
  over at Kôlias—, you couldn't get through the streets,
  what with the drums and the dancing. But now,
  not a woman in sight!
                    Except—oh, yes!
                              [*Enter* KALONIKE
  Here's one of my neighbors, at last. Good
  morning, Kalonikê.

7

KALONIKE:

Good morning, Lysistrata.

Darling,
don't frown so! You'll ruin your face!

LYSISTRATA:

Never mind my face.

Kalonikê,
the way we women behave! Really, I don't blame the men
for what they say about us.

KALONIKE:

No; I imagine they're right.

LYSISTRATA:

For example: I call a meeting
to think out a most important matter—and what hap-
pens?
The women all stay in bed!

KALONIKE:

Oh, they'll be along.
It's hard to get away, you know: a husband, a cook,
a child . . . Home life can be *so* demanding!

LYSISTRATA:

What I have in mind is even more demanding.

KALONIKE:

Tell me: what is it?

LYSISTRATA:

It's big.

KALONIKE:

Goodness! *How* big?

LYSISTRATA:

Big enough for all of us.

KALONIKE:

But we're not all here!

LYSISTRATA:

We would be, if *that*'s what was up!

No, Kalonikê,
this is something I've been turning over for nights,
long sleepless nights.

KALONIKE:

It must be getting worn down, then,
if you've spent so much time on it.

LYSISTRATA:
                                        Worn down or not,
it comes to this: Only we women can save Greece!
KALONIKE:
Only we women? Poor Greece!
LYSISTRATA:
                                        Just the same,
it's up to us. First, we must liquidate
the Peloponnesians—
KALONIKE:
                        Fun, fun!
LYSISTRATA:
                                        —and then the Boiotians.
KALONIKE:
Oh! But not those heavenly eels!
LYSISTRATA:
                                        You needn't worry.
I'm not talking about eels. —But here's the point:
If we can get the women from those places—
all those Boiotians and Peloponnesians—
to join us women here, why, we can save
all Greece!
KALONIKE:
                But dearest Lysistrata!
How can women do a thing so austere, so
political? We belong at home. Our only armor's
our perfumes, our saffron dresses and
our pretty little shoes!
LYSISTRATA:
                                Exactly. Those
transparent dresses, the saffron, the
perfume, those pretty shoes—
KALONIKE:
                                Oh?
LYSISTRATA:
                                        Not a single man would lift
his spear—
KALONIKE:
                I'll send my dress to the dyer's tomorrow!
LYSISTRATA:
—or grab a shield—

KALONIKE:

                    The sweetest little negligée—

LYSISTRATA:

  —or haul out his sword.

KALONIKE:

                I know where I can buy

the dreamiest sandals!

LYSISTRATA:

             Well, so you see. Now, shouldn't

the women have come?

KALONIKE:

                Come? They should have *flown!*

LYSISTRATA:

Athenians are always late.

              But imagine!

There's no one here from the South Shore, or from
    Sálamis.

KALONIKE:

Things are hard over in Sálamis, I swear.

They have to get going at dawn.

LYSISTRATA:

             And nobody from Acharnai.

I thought they'd be here hours ago.

KALONIKE:

               Well, you'll get

that awful Theagenês woman: she'll be
a sheet or so in the wind.

            But look!

Someone at last! Can you see who they are?

          [Enter MYRRHINE *and other women*

LYSISTRATA:

They're from Anagyros.

KALONIKE:

           They certainly are.

You'd know them anywhere, by the scent.

MYRRHINE:

Sorry to be late, Lysistrata.

         Oh come,

don't scowl so. Say something!

LYSISTRATA:

          My dear Myrrhinê,

what is there to say? After all,
you've been pretty casual about the whole thing.

MYRRHINE:

                                        Couldn't find
my girdle in the dark, that's all.

                              But what *is*
'the whole thing'?

KALONIKE:

                    No, we've got to wait
for those Boiotians and Peloponnesians.

LYSISTRATA:

That's more like it. —But, look!
Here's Lampitô!

                    [*Enter* LAMPITO *with women from Sparta*

LYSISTRATA:

                    Darling Lampitô,
how pretty you are today! What a nice color!
Goodness, you look as though you could strangle a bull!

LAMPITO:

Ah think Ah could! It's the work-out
in the gym every day; and, of co'se that dance of ahs
where y' kick yo' own tail.

KALONIKE:

                        What an adorable figure!

LAMPITO:

Lawdy, when y' touch me lahk that,
Ah feel lahk a heifer at the altar!

LYSISTRATA:

                              And this young lady?
Where is she from?

LAMPITO:

                    Boiotia. Social-Register type.

LYSISTRATA:

Ah. 'Boiotia of the fertile plain.'

KALONIKE:

                              And if you look,
you'll find the fertile plain has just been mowed.

LYSISTRATA:

And this lady?

LAMPITO:
                    Hagh, wahd, handsome. She comes from
    Korinth.
KALONIKE:
    High and wide's the 'word for it.
LAMPITO:
                            Which one of you
    called this heah meeting, and why?
LYSISTRATA:
                        I did.
LAMPITO:
                                Well, then, tell us:
    What's up?
MYRRHINE:
                    Yes, darling, what *is* on your mind, after all?
LYSISTRATA:
    I'll tell you. —But first, one little question.
MYRRHINE:
                                    Well?
LYSISTRATA:
    It's your husbands. Fathers of your children. Doesn't it
        bother you
    that they're always off with the Army? I'll stake my life,
    not one of you has a man in the house this minute!
KALONIKE:
    Mine's been in Thrace the last five months, keeping an eye
    on that General.
MYRRHINE:
                Mine's been in Pylos for seven.
LAMPITO:
                                And mahn,
    whenever he gets a *dis*charge, he goes raht back
    with that li'l ole shield of his, and enlists again!
LYSISTRATA:
    And not the ghost of a lover to be found!
    From the very day the war began—
                            those Milesians!
    I could skin them alive!
                        —I've not seen so much, even,
    as one of those leather consolation prizes.—

But there! What's important is: If I've found a way
to end the war, are you with me?

MYRRHINE:

                       I should *say* so!

Even if I have to pawn my best dress and
drink up the proceeds.

KALONIKE:

                  Me, too! Even if they split me
right up the middle, like a flounder.

LAMPITO:

                   Ah'm shorely with you.
Ah'd crawl up Taÿgetos on mah knees
if that'd bring peace.

LYSISTRATA:

            All right, then; here it is:

Women! Sisters!
If we really want our men to make peace,
we must be ready to give up—

MYRRHINE:

                Give up what?
Quick, tell us!

LYSISTRATA:

        But *will* you?

MYRRHINE:

                 We will, even if it kills us.

LYSISTRATA:

Then we must give up going to bed with our men.

                    [*Long silence*
Oh? So now you're sorry? Won't look at me?
Doubtful? Pale? All teary-eyed?

               But come: be frank with me.
Will you do it, or not? Well? Will you do it?

MYRRHINE:

                 I couldn't. No.
Let the war go on.

KALONIKE:

        Nor I. Let the war go on.

LYSISTRATA:

You, you little flounder,
ready to be split up the middle?

KALONIKE:

                          Lysistrata, no!
I'd walk through fire for you—you *know* I would!—, but
    don't
ask us to give up *that!* Why, there's nothing like it!

LYSISTRATA:

And you?

BOIOTIAN:

              No. I must say *I'd* rather walk through fire.

LYSISTRATA:

What an utterly perverted sex we women are!
No wonder poets write tragedies about us.
There's only one thing we can think of.

                        But you from Sparta:
if you stand by me, we may win yet! Will you?
It means so much!

LAMPITO:

             Ah sweah, it means *too* much!
By the Two Goddesses, it does! Asking a girl
to sleep—Heaven knows how long!—in a great big bed
with nobody there but herself! But Ah'll stay with you!
Peace comes first!

LYSISTRATA:

          Spoken like a true Spartan!

KALONIKE:

But if—
      oh dear!
          —if we give up what you tell us to,
will there *be* any peace?

LYSISTRATA:

             Why, mercy, of course there will!
We'll just sit snug in our very thinnest gowns,
perfumed and powdered from top to bottom, and those
    men
simply won't stand still! And when we say No,
they'll go out of their minds! And there's your peace.
You can take my word for it.

LAMPITO:

             Ah seem to remember
that Colonel Menelaos threw his sword away
when he saw Helen's breast all bare.

KALONIKE:

But, goodness me!
What if they just get up and leave us?

LYSISTRATA:

In that case
we'll have to fall back on ourselves, I suppose.
But they won't.

KALONIKE:

I must say that's not much help. But
what if they drag us into the bedroom?

LYSISTRATA:

Hang on to the door.

KALONIKE:

What if they slap us?

LYSISTRATA:

If they do, you'd better give in.
But be sulky about it. Do I have to teach you how?
You know there's no fun for men when they have to force
    you.
There are millions of ways of getting them to see reason.
Don't you worry: a man
doesn't like it unless the girl co-operates.

KALONIKE:

I suppose so. Oh, all right. We'll go along.

LAMPITO:

Ah imagine us Spahtans can arrange a peace. But you
Athenians! Why, you're just war-mongerers!

LYSISTRATA:

Leave that to me.
I know how to make them listen.

LAMPITO:

Ah don't see how.
After all, they've got their boats; and there's lots of money
piled up in the Akropolis.

LYSISTRATA:

The Akropolis? Darling,
we're taking over the Akropolis today!
That's the older women's job. All the rest of us
are going to the Citadel to sacrifice—you understand me?
And once there, we're in for good!

LAMPITO:

Whee! Up the rebels!
Ah can see you're a good strat*ee*gist.

L*'*SISTRATA:

Well, then, Lampitô,
what we have to do now is take a solemn oath.

LAMPITO:

Say it. We'll sweah.

LYSISTRATA:

This is it.
—But where's our Inner Guard?

—Look, Guard: you see this shield?
Put it down here. Now bring me the victim's entrails.

KALONIKE:

But the oath?

LYSISTRATA:

You remember how in Aischylos' *Seven*
they killed a sheep and swore on a shield? Well, then?

KALONIKE:

But I don't see how you can swear for peace on a shield.

LYSISTRATA:

What else do you suggest?

KALONIKE:

Why not a white horse?
We could swear by that.

LYSISTRATA:

And where will you get a white horse?

KALONIKE:

I never thought of that. *What* can we do?

LYSISTRATA:

I have it!
Let's set this big black wine-bowl on the ground
and pour in a gallon or so of Thasian, and swear
not to add one drop of water.

LAMPITO:

Ah lahk *that* oath!

LYSISTRATA:

Bring the bowl and the wine-jug.

KALONIKE:

Oh, what a simply *huge* one!

LYSISTRATA:

Set it down. Girls, place your hands on the gift-offering.

O Goddess of Persuasion! And thou, O Loving-cup:
Look upon this our sacrifice, and
be gracious!

KALONIKE:

See the blood spill out. How red and pretty it is!

LAMPITO:

And Ah must say it smells good.

MYRRHINE:

Let me swear first!

KALONIKE:

No, by Aphroditê, we'll match for it!

LYSISTRATA:

Lampitô: all of you women: come, touch the bowl,
and repeat after me—remember, this is an oath—:
I WILL HAVE NOTHING TO DO WITH MY HUS-
BAND OR MY LOVER

KALONIKE:

I will have nothing to do with my husband or my lover

LYSISTRATA:

THOUGH HE COME TO ME IN PITIABLE CONDI-
TION

KALONIKE:

Though he come to me in pitiable condition
(Oh Lysistrata! This is killing me!)

LYSISTRATA:

IN MY HOUSE I WILL BE UNTOUCHABLE

KALONIKE:

In my house I will be untouchable

LYSISTRATA:

IN MY THINNEST SAFFRON SILK

KALONIKE:

In my thinnest saffron silk

LYSISTRATA:

AND MAKE HIM LONG FOR ME.

KALONIKE:

And make him long for me.

LYSISTRATA:

I WILL NOT GIVE MYSELF

KALONIKE:
I will not give myself

LYSISTRATA:
AND IF HE CONSTRAINS ME

KALONIKE:
And if he constrains me

LYSISTRATA:
I WILL BE COLD AS ICE AND NEVER MOVE

KALONIKE:
I will be cold as ice and never move

LYSISTRATA:
I WILL NOT LIFT MY SLIPPERS TOWARD THE CEILING

KALONIKE:
I will not lift my slippers toward the ceiling

LYSISTRATA:
OR CROUCH ON ALL FOURS LIKE THE LIONESS IN THE CARVING

KALONIKE:
Or crouch on all fours like the lioness in the carving

LYSISTRATA:
AND IF I KEEP THIS OATH LET ME DRINK FROM THIS BOWL

KALONIKE:
And if I keep this oath let me drink from this bowl

LYSISTRATA:
IF NOT, LET MY OWN BOWL BE FILLED WITH WATER.

KALONIKE:
If not, let my own bowl be filled with water.

LYSISTRATA:
You have all sworn?

MYRRHINE:
We have.

LYSISTRATA:
Then thus
I sacrifice the victim.

[Drinks largely

KALONIKE:
Save some for us!
Here's to you, darling, and to you, and to you!

[*Loud cries off-stage*

LAMPITO:
What's all *that* whoozy-goozy?
LYSISTRATA:
Just what I told you.
The older women have taken the Akropolis.
Now you, Lampitô,
rush back to Sparta. We'll take care of things here. Leave
these girls here for hostages.
The rest of you,
up to the Citadel: and mind you push in the bolts.
KALONIKE:
But the men? Won't they be after us?
LYSISTRATA:
Just you leave
the men to me. There's not fire enough in the world,
or threats either, to make me open these doors
except on my own terms.
KALONIKE:
I hope not, by Aphroditê!
After all,
we've got a reputation for bitchiness to live up to.

[*Exeunt*

PÁRODOS: CHORAL EPISODE

[*The hillside just under the Akropolis. Enter*
CHORUS OF OLD MEN *with burning torches and*
braziers; much puffing and coughing

KORYPHAIOS[m]:
Forward march, Drakês, old friend: never you mind
that damn big log banging hell down on your back.

CHORUS[m]:
There's this to be said for longevity: [STROPHE 1
You see things you thought that you'd never see.
Look, Strymodôros, who would have thought it?
We've caught it—
the New Femininity!
The wives of our bosom, our board, our bed—

Now, by the gods, they've gone ahead
And taken the Citadel (Heaven knows why!),
Profanèd the sacred statuar-y,

And barred the doors,
The subversive whores!

KORYPHAIOS^m:

Shake a leg there, Philûrgos, man: the Akropolis or
bust!
Put the kindling around here. We'll build one almighty
big
bonfire for the whole bunch of bitches, every last one;
and the first we fry will be old Lykôn's woman.

CHORUS^m:

[ANTISTROPHE 1
They're not going to give me the old horse-laugh!
No, by Deméter, they won't pull this off!
Think of Kleómenês: even he
Didn't go free
till he brought me his stuff.
A good man he was, all stinking and shaggy,
Bare as an eel except for the bag he
Covered his rear with. God, what a mess!
Never a bath in six years, I'd guess.
Pure Sparta, man!
He also ran.

KORYPHAIOS^m:

That was a siege, friends! Seventeen ranks strong
we slept at the Gate. And shall we not do as much
against these women, whom God and Euripides hate?
If we don't, I'll turn in my medals from Marathon.

Not very strong

CHORUS^m:

[STROPHE 2
Onward and upward! A little push,
And we're there.
Ouch, my shoulders! I could wish
For a pair

Of good strong oxen. Keep your eye
   On the fire there, it mustn't die.
      Akh! Akh!
   The smoke would make a cadaver cough!

Holy Heraklês, a hot spark   [ANTISTROPHE 2
   Bit my eye!
Damn this hellfire, damn this work!
   So say I.
Onward and upward just the same.
(Lachês, remember the Goddess: for shame!)
      Akh! Akh!
   The smoke would make a cadaver cough!

KORYPHAIOS^m:

At last (and let us give suitable thanks to God
for his infinite mercies) I have managed to bring
my personal flame to the common goal. It breathes, it
      lives.
Now, gentlemen, let us consider. Shall we insert
the torch, say, into the brazier, and thus extract
a kindling brand? And shall we then, do you think,
push on to the gate like valiant sheep? On the whole, yes.
But I would have you consider this, too: if they—
I refer to the women—should refuse to open,
what then? Do we set the doors afire
and smoke them out? At ease, men. Meditate.
Akh, the smoke! Woof! What we really need
is the loan of a general or two from the Samos Command.
At least we've got this lumber off our backs.
That's something. And now let's look to our fire.

O Pot, brave Brazier, touch my torch with flame!
Victory, Goddess, I invoke thy name!
Strike down these paradigms of female pride,
And we shall hang our trophies up inside.
            [Enter CHORUS OF OLD WOMEN on the walls of the
            Akropolis, carrying jars of water

KORYPHAIOS^w:

Smoke, girls, smoke! There's smoke all over the place!
Probably fire, too. Hurry, girls! Fire! Fire!

CHORUS^W:

Nikodikê, run!   [STROPHE 1
Or Kalykê's done
To a turn, and poor Kritylla's
Smoked like a ham.
                    Damn
These old men! Are we too late?
I nearly died down at the place
Where we fill our jars:
     Slaves pushing and jostling—
     Such a hustling
I never saw in all my days.

But here's water at last.   [ANTISTROPHE 1
Haste, sisters, haste!
Slosh it on them, slosh it down,
The silly old wrecks!
                    Sex
Almighty! What they want's
A hot bath? Good. Send one down.
Athêna of Athens town,
     Trito-born! Helm of Gold!
     Cripple the old
Firemen! Help us help them drown!

          [*The* OLD MEN *capture a woman,* STRATYLLIS

STRATYLLIS:
  Let me go! Let me go!
KORYPHAIOS^W:
                    You walking corpses,
  have you no shame?
KORYPHAIOS^m:
                    I wouldn't have believed it!
  An army of women in the Akropolis!
KORYPHAIOS^W:
  So we scare you, do we? Grandpa, you've seen
  only our pickets yet!
KORYPHAIOS^m:
                    Hey, Phaidrias!
  Help me with the necks of these jabbering hens!

KORYPHAIOS^w:
Down with your pots, girls! We'll need both hands
if these antiques attack us.
KORYPHAIOS^m:
                                        Want your face kicked in?

KORYPHAIOS^w:
Want your balls chewed off?
KORYPHAIOS^m:
                                        Look out! I've got a stick!

KORYPHAIOS^w:
You lay a half-inch of your stick on Stratyllis,
and you'll never stick again!
KORYPHAIOS^m:
Fall apart!
KORYPHAIOS^w:
              I'll spit up your guts!
KORYPHAIOS^m:
                                        Euripides! Master!
How well you knew women!
KORYPHAIOS^w:
                                        Listen to him! Rhodippê,
up with the pots!
KORYPHAIOS^m:
                        Demolition of God,
what good are your pots?
KORYPHAIOS^w:
                                You refugee from the tomb,
what good is your fire?
KORYPHAIOS^m:
                                Good enough to make a pyre
to barbecue you!
KORYPHAIOS^w:
                                We'll squizzle your kindling!

KORYPHAIOS^m:
You think so?
KORYPHAIOS^w:
                        Yah! Just hang around a while!
KORYPHAIOS^m:
Want a touch of my torch?
KORYPHAIOS^w:
                                It needs a good soaping.

KORYPHAIOS^m:
How about you?

KORYPHAIOS^w:
Soap for a senile bridegroom!

KORYPHAIOS^m:
Senile? Hold your trap!

KORYPHAIOS^w:
Just *you* try to hold it!

KORYPHAIOS^m:
The yammer of women!

KORYPHAIOS^w:
Oh is that so?
You're not in the jury room now, you know.

KORYPHAIOS^m:
Gentlemen, I beg you, burn off that woman's hair!

KORYPHAIOS^w:
Let it come down!

[*They empty their pots on the men*

KORYPHAIOS^m:
What a way to drown!

KORYPHAIOS^w:
Hot, hey?

KORYPHAIOS^m:
Say,
enough!

KORYPHAIOS^w:
Dandruff
needs watering. I'll make you
nice and fresh.

KORYPHAIOS^m:
For God's sake, you,
hold off!

🎭 SCENE I

[*Enter a* COMMISSIONER *accompanied by four con-stables*

COMMISSIONER:
These degenerate women! What a racket of little drums,
what a yapping for Adonis on every house-top!

It's like the time in the Assembly when I was listening
to a speech—out of order, as usual—by that fool
Demostratos, all about troops for Sicily,
that kind of nonsense—
                                    and there was his wife
trotting around in circles howling
Alas for Adonis!—
                              and Demostratos insisting
we must draft every last Zakynthian that can walk—
and his wife up there on the roof,
drunk as an owl, yowling
Oh weep for Adonis!—
                                    and that damned ox Demostratos
mooing away through the rumpus. That's what we get
for putting up with this wretched woman-business!

KORYPHAIOS[m]:

Sir, you haven't heard the half of it. They laughed at us!
Insulted us! They took pitchers of water
and nearly drowned us! We're still wringing out our
     clothes,
for all the world like unhousebroken brats.

COMMISSIONER:

Serves you right, by Poseidon!
Whose fault is it if these women-folk of ours
get out of hand? We coddle them,
we teach them to be wasteful and loose. You'll see a hus-
     band
go into a jeweler's. 'Look,' he'll say,
'jeweler,' he'll say, 'you remember that gold choker
'you made for my wife? Well, she went to a dance last
     night
'and broke the clasp. Now, I've got to go to Sálamis,
'and can't be bothered. Run over to my house tonight,
'will you, and see if you can put it together for her.'
Or another one
goes to a cobbler—a good strong workman, too,
with an awl that was never meant for child's play. 'Here,'
he'll tell him, 'one of my wife's shoes is pinching
'her little toe. Could you come up about noon
'and stretch it out for her?'
                                    Well, what do you expect?

Look at me, for example. I'm a Public Officer,
and it's one of my duties to pay off the sailors.
And where's the money? Up there in the Akropolis!
And those blasted women slam the door in my face!
But what are we waiting for?

        —Look here, constable,
stop sniffing around for a tavern, and get us
some crowbars. We'll force their gates! As a matter of
    fact,
I'll do a little forcing myself.

        [*Enter* LYSISTRATA, *above, with* MYRRHINE, KALO-
        NIKE, *and the* BOIOTIAN

LYSISTRATA:

        No need of forcing.
Here I am, of my own accord. And all this talk
about locked doors—! We don't need locked doors,
but just the least bit of common sense.

COMMISSIONER:

Is that so, ma'am!

        —Where's my constable?

        —Constable,
arrest that woman, and tie her hands behind her.

LYSISTRATA:

If he touches me, I swear by Artemis
there'll be one scamp dropped from the public pay-roll
    tomorrow!

COMMISSIONER:

Well, constable? You're not afraid, I suppose? Grab her,
two of you, around the middle!

KALONIKE:

        No, by Pándrosos!
Lay a hand on her, and I'll jump on you so hard
your guts will come out the back door!

COMMISSIONER:

        That's what *you* think!
Where's the sergeant?—Here, you: tie up that trollop
    first,
the one with the pretty talk!

MYRRHINE:

        By the Moon-Goddess,
just try! They'll have to scoop you up with a spoon!

COMMISSIONER:
Another one!

               Officer, seize that woman!

                                 I swear
I'll put an end to this riot!

BOIOTIAN:

                      By the Taurian,
one inch closer, you'll be one screaming bald-head!

COMMISSIONER:
Lord, what a mess! And my constables seem ineffective.
But—women get the best of us? By God, no!

                            —Skythians!
Close ranks and forward march!

LYSISTRATA:

                      'Forward,' indeed!
By the Two Goddesses, what's the sense in *that*?
They're up against four companies of women
armed from top to bottom.

COMMISSIONER:

                  Forward, my Skythians!

LYSISTRATA:
Forward, yourselves, dear comrades!
You grainlettucebeanseedmarket girls!
You garlicandonionbreadbakery girls!
Give it to 'em! Knock 'em down! Scratch 'em!
Tell 'em what you think of 'em!

                [*General mêlée; the Skythians yield*
                    —Ah, that's enough!
Sound a retreat: good soldiers don't rob the dead.

COMMISSIONER:
A nice day *this* has been for the police!

LYSISTRATA:
Well, there you are.—Did you really think we women
would be driven like slaves? Maybe now you'll admit
that a woman knows something about spirit.

COMMISSIONER:

                         Spirit enough,
especially spirits in bottles! Dear Lord Apollo!

KORYPHAIOS[m]:
Your Honor, there's no use talking to them. Words
mean nothing whatever to wild animals like these.

Think of the sousing they gave us! and the water
was not, I believe, of the purest.

KORYPHAIOS^w:

You shouldn't have come after us. And if you try it again,
you'll be one eye short!—Although, as a matter of fact,
what I like best is just to stay at home and read,
like a sweet little bride: never hurting a soul, no,
never going out. But if you *must* shake hornets' nests,
look out for the hornets.

CHORUS^m:

Of all the beasts that God hath wrought   [STROPHE 1
    What monster's worse than woman?
Who shall encompass with his thought
    Their guile unending? No man.

They've seized the Heights, the Rock, the Shrine—
    But to what end? I wot not.
Sure there's some clue to their design!
    Have you the key? I thought not.

KORYPHAIOS^m:

We might question them, I suppose. But I warn you, sir,
don't believe anything you hear! It would be un-Athenian
not to get to the bottom of this plot.

COMMISSIONER:

                                    Very well.
My first question is this: Why, so help you God,
did you bar the gates of the Akropolis?

LYSISTRATA:

                                    Why?
To keep the money, of course. No money, no war.

COMMISSIONER:

You think that money's the cause of war?

LYSISTRATA:

                                    I do.
Money brought about that Peisandros business
and all the other attacks on the State. Well and good!
They'll not get another cent here!

COMMISSIONER:

                        And what will you do?

LYSISTRATA:

What a question! From now on, we intend
to control the Treasury.

COMMISSIONER:

Control the Treasury!

LYSISTRATA:

Why not? Does that seem strange? After all,
we control our household budgets.

COMMISSIONER:

But that's different!

LYSISTRATA:

'Different'? What do you mean?

COMMISSIONER:

I mean simply this:
it's the Treasury that pays for National Defense.

LYSISTRATA:

Unnecessary. We propose to abolish war.

COMMISSIONER:

Good God.—And National Security?

LYSISTRATA:

Leave that to us.

COMMISSIONER:

You?

LYSISTRATA:

Us.

COMMISSIONER:

We're done for, then!

LYSISTRATA:

Never mind.
We women will save you in spite of yourselves.

COMMISSIONER:

What nonsense!

LYSISTRATA:

If you like. But you must accept it, like it or not.

COMMISSIONER:

Why, this is downright subversion!

LYSISTRATA:

Maybe it is.
But we're going to save you, Judge.

COMMISSIONER:

I don't *want* to be saved.

LYSISTRATA:

Tut. The death-wish. All the more reason.

COMMISSIONER:

But the idea
of women bothering themselves about peace and war!

LYSISTRATA:

Will you listen to me?

COMMISSIONER:

Yes. But be brief, or I'll—

LYSISTRATA:

This is no time for stupid threats.

COMMISSIONER:

By the gods,
I can't stand any more!

AN OLD WOMAN:

Can't stand? Well, well.

COMMISSIONER:

That's enough out of you, you old buzzard!
Now, Lysistrata: tell me what you're thinking.

LYSISTRATA:

Glad to.

Ever since this war began
We women have been watching you men, agreeing with
you,
keeping our thoughts to ourselves. That doesn't mean
we were happy: we weren't, for we saw how things were
going;
but we'd listen to you at dinner
arguing this way and that.

—Oh you, and your big

Top Secrets!—

And then we'd grin like little patriots
(though goodness knows we didn't feel like grinning) and
ask you:
'Dear, did the Armistice come up in Assembly today?'
And you'd say, 'None of your business! Pipe down!',
you'd say.
And so we would.

AN OLD WOMAN:

I wouldn't have, by God!

COMMISSIONER:

You'd have taken a beating, then!

—Go on.

LYSISTRATA:

Well, we'd be quiet. But then, you know, all at once
you men would think up something worse than ever.
Even *I* could see it was fatal. And, 'Darling,' I'd say,
'have you gone completely mad?' And my husband would
    look at me
and say, 'Wife, you've got your weaving to attend to.
'Mind your tongue, if you don't want a slap. "War's
' "a man's affair"'!'
COMMISSIONER:

                Good words, and well pronounced.

LYSISTRATA:

You're a fool if you think so.

                  It was hard enough
to put up with all this banquet-hall strategy.
But then we'd hear you out in the public square:
'Nobody left for the draft-quota here in Athens?'
you'd say; and, 'No,' someone else would say, 'not a man!'
And so we women decided to rescue Greece.
You might as well listen to us now: you'll have to, later.

COMMISSIONER:

You rescue Greece? Absurd.

LYSISTRATA:

                You're the absurd one.

COMMISSIONER:

You expect me to take orders from a woman?

                      I'd die first!

LYSISTRATA:

Heavens, if that's what's bothering you, take my veil,
here, and wrap it around your poor head.

KALONIKE:

                          Yes,
and you can have my market-basket, too.
Go home, tighten your girdle, do the washing, mind
your beans! 'War's
a woman's affair'!

KORYPHAIOS^W:

             Ground pitchers! Close ranks!

CHORUS^w:

[ANTISTROPHE

This is a dance that I know well,
    My knees shall never yield.
Wobble and creak I may, but still
    I'll keep the well-fought field.

Valor and grace march on before,
    Love prods us from behind.
Our slogan is EXCELSIOR,
    Our watchword SAVE MANKIND.

KORYPHAIOS^w:

Women, remember your grandmothers! Remember
that little old mother of yours, what a stinger she was!
On, on, never slacken. There's a strong wind astern!

LYSISTRATA:

O Erôs of delight! O Aphroditê! Kyprian!
If ever desire has drenched our breasts or dreamed
in our thighs, let it work so now on the men of Hellas
that they shall tail us through the land, slaves, slaves
to Woman, Breaker of Armies!

COMMISSIONER:

And if we do?

LYSISTRATA:

Well, for one thing, we shan't have to watch you
going to market, a spear in one hand, and heaven knows
what in the other.

KALONIKE:

Nicely said, by Aphroditê!

LYSISTRATA:

As things stand now, you're neither men nor women.
Armor clanking with kitchen pans and pots—
you sound like a pack of Korybantês!

COMMISSIONER:

A man must do what a man must do.

LYSISTRATA:

So I'm told.

But to see a General, complete with Gorgon-shield,
jingling along the dock to buy a couple of herrings!

KALONIKE:

I saw a Captain the other day —lovely fellow he was,

nice curly hair—sitting on his horse; and—can you believe it?—
he'd just bought some soup, and was pouring it into his
helmet!
And there was a soldier from Thrace
swishing his lance like something out of Euripides,
and the poor fruit-store woman got so scared
that she ran away and let him have his figs free!

COMMISSIONER:
All this is beside the point.

Will you be so kind
as to tell me how you mean to save Greece?

LYSISTRATA:

Of course.
Nothing could be simpler.

COMMISSIONER:

I assure you, I'm all ears.

LYSISTRATA:
Do you know anything about weaving?
Say the yarn gets tangled: we thread it
this way and that through the skein, up and down,
until it's free. And it's like that with war.
We'll send our envoys
up and down, this way and that, all over Greece,
until it's finished.

COMMISSIONER:

Yarn? Thread? Skein?
Are you out of your mind? I tell you,
war is a serious business.

LYSISTRATA:

So serious
that I'd like to go on talking about weaving.

COMMISSIONER:
All right. Go ahead.

LYSISTRATA:

The first thing we have to do
is to wash our yarn, get the dirt out of it.
You see? Isn't there too much dirt here in Athens?
You must wash those men away.

Then our spoiled wool—
that's like your job-hunters, out for a life

of no work and big pay. Back to the basket,
citizens or not, allies or not,
or friendly immigrants.

And your colonies?
Hanks of wool lost in various places. Pull them
together, weave them into one great whole,
and our voters are clothed for ever.

COMMISSIONER:

It would take a woman
to reduce state questions to a matter of carding and
weaving.

LYSISTRATA:

You fool! Who were the mothers whose sons sailed off
to fight for Athens in Sicily?

COMMISSIONER:

Enough!
I beg you, do not call back those memories.

LYSISTRATA:

And then,
instead of the love that every woman needs,
we have only our single beds, where we can dream
of our husbands off with the Army.

Bad enough for wives!
But what about our girls, getting older every day,
and older, and no kisses?

COMMISSIONER:

Men get older, too.

LYSISTRATA:

Not in the same sense.

A soldier's discharged,
and he may be bald and toothless, yet he'll find
a pretty young thing to go to bed with.

But a woman!
Her beauty is gone with the first grey hair.
She can spend her time
consulting the oracles and the fortune-tellers,
but they'll never send her a husband.

COMMISSIONER:

Still, if a man can rise to the occasion—

LYSISTRATA:
Rise? Rise, yourself!

[*Furiously*

Go invest in a coffin!

You've money enough.

I'll bake you
a cake for the Underworld.

And here's your funeral
wreath!

[*She pours water upon him*

MYRRHINE:
And here's another!

[*More water*

KALONIKE:

And here's
my contribution!

[*More water*

LYSISTRATA:
What are you waiting for?
All aboard Styx Ferry!

Charôn's calling for you!
It's sailing-time: don't disrupt the schedule!

COMMISSIONER:
The insolence of women! And to me!
No, by God, I'll go back to town and show
the rest of the Commission what might happen to them.

[*Exit* COMMISSIONER

LYSISTRATA:
Really, I suppose we should have laid out his corpse
on the doorstep, in the usual way.

But never mind.
We'll give him the rites of the dead tomorrow morning.

[*Exit* LYSISTRATA *with* MYRRHINE *and* KALONIKE

🎭 PARÁBASIS: CHORAL EPISODE

KORYPHAIOS[m]:

[ODE 1
Sons of Liberty, awake! The day of glory is at hand.

CHORUS^m:

I smell tyranny afoot, I smell it rising from the land.
I scent a trace of Hippias, I sniff upon the breeze
A dismal Spartan hogo that suggests King Kleisthenês.
 Strip, strip for action, brothers!
 Our wives, aunts, sisters, mothers
Have sold us out: the streets are full of godless female
 rages.
Shall we stand by and let our women confiscate our wages?

KORYPHAIOS^m:

[EPIRRHEMA 1

Gentlemen, it's a disgrace to Athens, a disgrace
to all that Athens stands for, if we allow these grandmas
to jabber about spears and shields and making friends
with the Spartans. What's a Spartan? Give me a wild wolf
any day. No. They want the Tyranny back, I suppose.
Are we going to take that? No. Let us look like
the innocent serpent, but be the flower under it,
as the poet sings. And just to begin with,
I propose to poke a number of teeth
down the gullet of that harridan over there.

KORYPHAIOS^w:

[ANTODE 1

Oh, is that so? When you get home, your own mammá
 won't know you!

CHORUS^w:

Who do you think we are, you senile bravos? Well, I'll
 show you.
I bore the sacred vessels in my eighth year, and at ten
I was pounding out the barley for Athêna Goddess; then
 They made me Little Bear
 At the Braunonian Fair;
I'd held the Holy Basket by the time I was of age,
The Blessed Dry Figs had adorned my plump décolletage.

KORYPHAIOS^w:

[ANTEPIRRHEMA 1

A 'disgrace to Athens', am I, just at the moment
I'm giving Athens the best advice she ever had?

Don't I pay taxes to the State? Yes, I pay them
in baby boys. And what do you contribute,
you impotent horrors? Nothing but waste: all
our Treasury, dating back to the Persian Wars,
gone! rifled! And not a penny out of your pockets!
Well, then? Can you cough up an answer to that?
Look out for your own gullet, or you'll get a crack
from this old brogan that'll make your teeth see stars!

CHORUS^m:

                Oh insolence!   [ODE 2
                Am I unmanned?
                Incontinence!
                Shall my scarred hand
                Strike never a blow
                To curb this flow-
                ing female curse?

                Leipsydrion!
                Shall I betray
                The laurels won
                On that great day?
                Come, shake a leg,
                Shed old age, beg
                The years reverse!

KORYPHAIOS^m:

                                 [EPIRRHEMA 2
Give them an inch, and we're done for! We'll have them
launching boats next and planning naval strategy,
sailing down on us like so many Artemisias.
Or maybe they have ideas about the cavalry.
That's fair enough, women are certainly good
in the saddle. Just look at Mikôn's paintings,
all those Amazons wrestling with all those men!
On the whole, a straitjacket's their best uniform.

CHORUS^w:

              /Tangle with me,   [ANTODE 2
             / And you'll get cramps.
             Ferocity

C

's no use now, Gramps!
By the Two,
I'll get through
To you wrecks yet!

I'll scramble your eggs,
I'll burn your beans,
With my two legs.
You'll see such scenes
As never yet
Your two eyes met.
A curse? You bet!

KORYPHAIOS^w:

[ANTEPIRRHEMA 2
If Lampitô stands by me, and that delicious Theban girl,
Ismênia—what good are *you*? You and your seven
Resolutions! Resolutions? Rationing Boiotian eels
and making our girls go without them at Hekatê's Feast!
That was statesmanship! And we'll have to put up with it
and all the rest of your decrepit legislation
until some patriot—God give him strength!—
grabs you by the neck and kicks you off the Rock.

✥ SCENE II

[*Re-enter* LYSISTRATA *and her lieutenants*

KORYPHAIOS^w [*Tragic tone*]:
    Great Queen, fair Architect of our emprise,
    Why lookst thou on us with foreboding eyes?

LYSISTRATA:
    The behavior of these idiotic women!
    There's something about the female temperament
    that I can't bear!
KORYPHAIOS^w:
                    What in the world do you mean?
LYSISTRATA:
    Exactly what I say.

KORYPHAIOS^w:

What dreadful thing has happened?
Come, tell us: we're all your friends.

LYSISTRATA:

It isn't easy
to say it; yet, God knows, we can't hush it up.

KORYPHAIOS^w:

Well, then? Out with it!

LYSISTRATA:

To put it bluntly,
we're dying to get laid.

KORYPHAIOS^w:

Almighty God!

LYSISTRATA:

Why bring God into it?—No, it's just as I say.
I can't manage them any longer: they've gone man-crazy,
they're all trying to get out.

Why, look:
one of them was sneaking out the back door
over there by Pan's cave; another
was sliding down the walls with rope and tackle;
another was climbing aboard a sparrow, ready to take off
for the nearest brothel—I dragged *her* back by the hair!
They're all finding some reason to leave.

Look there!

There goes another one.

—Just a minute, you!
Where are you off to so fast?

FIRST WOMAN:

I've got to get home.
I've a lot of Milesian wool, and the worms are spoiling it.

LYSISTRATA:

Oh bother you and your worms! Get back inside!

FIRST WOMAN:

I'll be back right away, I swear I will.
I just want to get it stretched out on my bed.

LYSISTRATA:

You'll do no such thing. You'll stay right here.

FIRST WOMAN:

And my wool?

You want it ruined?

LYSISTRATA:

Yes, for all I care.

SECOND WOMAN:

Oh dear! My lovely new flax from Amorgos—
I left it at home, all uncarded!

LYSISTRATA:

Another one!
And all she wants is someone to card her flax.
Get back in there!

SECOND WOMAN:

But I swear by the Moon-Goddess,
the minute I get it done, I'll be back!

LYSISTRATA:

I say No.
If you, why not all the other women as well?

THIRD WOMAN:

O Lady Eileithyia! Radiant goddess! Thou
intercessor for women in childbirth! Stay, I pray thee,
oh stay this parturition. Shall I pollute
a sacred spot?

LYSISTRATA:

And what's the matter with *you*?

THIRD WOMAN:

I'm having a baby—any minute now.

LYSISTRATA:

But you weren't pregnant yesterday.

THIRD WOMAN:

Well, I am today.
Let me go home for a midwife, Lysistrata:
there's not much time.

LYSISTRATA:

I never heard such nonsense.
What's that bulging under your cloak?

THIRD WOMAN:

A little baby boy.

LYSISTRATA:

It certainly isn't. But it's something hollow,
like a basin or— Why, it's the helmet of Athêna!
And you said you were having a baby.

THIRD WOMAN:

Well, I am! So there!

LYSISTRATA:
Then why the helmet?
THIRD WOMAN:
I was afraid that my pains
might begin here in the Akropolis; and I wanted
to drop my chick into it, just as the dear doves do.
LYSISTRATA:
Lies! Evasions!—But at least one thing's clear:
you can't leave the place before your purification.
THIRD WOMAN:
But I can't stay here in the Akropolis! Last night I
    dreamed
of the Snake.
FIRST WOMAN:
And those horrible owls, the noise they make!
I can't get a bit of sleep; I'm just about dead.
LYSISTRATA:
You useless girls, that's enough: Let's have no more lying.
Of course you want your men. But don't you imagine
that they want you just as much? I'll give you my word,
their nights must be pretty hard.
Just stick it out!
A little patience, that's all, and our battle's won.
I have heard an Oracle. Should you like to hear it?
FIRST WOMAN:
An Oracle? Yes, tell us!
LYSISTRATA:
Here is what it says:
WHEN SWALLOWS SHALL THE HOOPOE SHUN
    AND SPURN HIS HOT DESIRE,
ZEUS WILL PERFECT WHAT THEY'VE BEGUN
    AND SET THE LOWER HIGHER.
FIRST WOMAN:
Does that mean we'll be on top?
LYSISTRATA:
BUT IF THE SWALLOWS SHALL FALL OUT
    AND TAKE THE HOOPOE'S BAIT,
A CURSE MUST MARK THEIR HOUR OF DOUBT,
    INFAMY SEAL THEIR FATE.
THIRD WOMAN:
I swear, *that* Oracle's all too clear.

FIRST WOMAN:

Oh the dear gods!

LYSISTRATA:

Let's not be downhearted, girls. Back to our places!
The god has spoken. How can we possibly fail him?
                    [*Exit* LYSISTRATA *with the dissident women*

CHORAL EPISODE

CHORUS^m: *statement or ques^n*

angela
                                                [STROPHE
I know a little story that I learned way back in school
Goes like this:
Once upon a time there was a young man—and no fool—
Named Melanion; and his
One aversi-on was marriage. He loathed the very thought.
So he ran off to the hills, and in a special grot
Raised a dog, and spent his days
Hunting rabbits. And it says
That he never never never did come home.
It might be called a refuge *from* the womb.
All right,
            all right,
                        all right!
We're as bright as young Melanion, and we hate the very
    sight
Of you women!

                            Possible movement
A MAN: *duo. along side*
How about a kiss, old lady?   *the actors.*
A WOMAN:
Here's an onion for your eye!
A MAN:
A kick in the guts, then?
A WOMAN:
Try, old bristle-tail, just try!
A MAN:
Yet they say Myronidês
On hands and knees
Looked just as shaggy fore and aft as I!

CHORUS[w]:

responce~ answer [ANTISTROPHE

Well, *I* know a little story, and it's just as good as yours.
Goes like this:
Once there was a man named Timon—a rough diamond,
    of course,
And that whiskery face of his
Looked like murder in the shrubbery. By God, he was a
    son
Of the Furies, let me tell you! And what did he do but run
From the world and all its ways,
Cursing mankind! And it says
That his choicest execrations as of then
Were leveled almost wholly at *old* men.
All right,
        all right,
            all right!
But there's one thing about Timon: he could always stand
    the sight
Of us women.

A WOMAN:
How about a crack in the jaw, Pop?
A MAN:
I can take it, Ma—no fear!
A WOMAN:
How about a kick in the face?
A MAN:
You'd reveal your old caboose?
A WOMAN:
What I'd show,
I'll have you know,
Is an instrument you're too far gone to use.

 SCENE III

[*Re-enter* LYSISTRATA

LYSISTRATA:
Oh, quick, girls, quick! Come here!

A WOMAN:

What is it?

LYSISTRATA:

A man.

A man simply bulging with love.

O Kyprian Queen,
O Paphian, O Kythereian! Hear us and aid us!

A WOMAN:
Where is this enemy?

LYSISTRATA:

Over there, by Demêter's shrine.

A WOMAN:
Damned if he isn't. But who *is* he?

MYRRHINE:

My husband.

Kinêsias.

LYSISTRATA:

Oh then, get busy! Tease him! Undermine him!
Wreck him! Give him everything—kissing, tickling,
nudging,
whatever you generally torture him with—: give him
everything
except what we swore on the wine we would not give.

MYRRHINE:
Trust me.

LYSISTRATA:

I do. But I'll help you get him started.
The rest of you women, stay back.

[*Enter* KINESIAS

KINESIAS:

Oh God! Oh my God!
I'm stiff from lack of exercise. All I can do to stand up.

LYSISTRATA:
Halt! Who are you, approaching our lines?

KINESIAS:

Me? I.

LYSISTRATA:
A man?

KINESIAS:

You have eyes, haven't you?

LYSISTRATA:

Go away.

KINESIAS:

Who says so?

LYSISTRATA:

Officer of the Day.

KINESIAS:

Officer, I beg you,
by all the gods at once, bring Myrrhinê out.

LYSISTRATA:

Myrrhinê? And who, my good sir, are you?

KINESIAS:

Kinêsias. Last name's Pennison. Her husband.

LYSISTRATA:

Oh, of course. I beg your pardon. We're glad to see you.
We've heard so much about you. Dearest Myrrhinê
is always talking about 'Kinêsias'—never nibbles an egg
or an apple without saying
'Here's to Kinêsias!'

KINESIAS:

Do you really mean it?

LYSISTRATA:

I do.

When we're discussing men, she always says
'Well, after all, there's nobody like Kinêsias!'

KINESIAS:

Good God.—Well, then, please send her down here.

LYSISTRATA:

And what do *I* get out of it?

KINESIAS:

A standing promise.

LYSISTRATA:

I'll take it up with her.

[*Exit* LYSISTRATA

KINESIAS:

But be quick about it!
Lord, what's life without a wife? Can't eat. Can't sleep.
Every time I go home, the place is so empty, so
insufferably sad. Love's killing me. Oh,
hurry!

[Enter MANES, *a slave, with* KINESIAS' *baby; the voice of* MYRRHINE *is heard off-stage.*

MYRRHINE:

But of course I love him! Adore him!—But no, he hates love. No. I won't go down.

[Enter MYRRHINE, *above*

KINESIAS:

Myrrhinê!

Darlingest Myrrhinette! Come down quick!

MYRRHINE:

Certainly not.

KINESIAS:

Not? But why, Myrrhinê?

MYRRHINE:

Why? You don't need me.

KINESIAS:

Need you? My God, *look* at me!

MYRRHINE:

So long!

[Turns to go

KINESIAS:

Myrrhinê, Myrrhinê, Myrrhinê!

If not for my sake, for our child!

[Pinches BABY
—All right, you: pipe up!

BABY:

Mummie! Mummie! Mummie!

KINESIAS:

You hear that?

Pitiful, I call it. Six days now

with never a bath; no food; enough to break your heart!

MYRRHINE:

My darlingest child! What a father *you* acquired!

KINESIAS:

At least come down for his sake.

MYRRHINE:

I suppose I must.

Oh, this mother business!

[Exit

KINESIAS:

How pretty she is! And younger!

The harder she treats me, the more bothered I get.

[MYRRHINE *enters, below*

MYRRHINE:

Dearest child,
you're as sweet as your father's horrid. Give me a kiss.

KINESIAS:

Now don't you see how wrong it was to get involved
in this scheming League of women? It's bad
for us both.

MYRRHINE:

Keep your hands to yourself!

KINESIAS:

But our house
going to rack and ruin?

MYRRHINE:

I don't care.

KINESIAS:

And your knitting
all torn to pieces by the chickens? Don't you care?

MYRRHINE:

Not at all.

KINESIAS:

And our debt to Aphroditê?
Oh, *won't* you come back?

MYRRHINE:

No.—At least, not until you men
make a treaty and stop this war.

KINESIAS:

Why, I suppose
that might be arranged.

MYRRHINE:

Oh? Well, I suppose
I might come down then. But meanwhile,
I've sworn not to.

KINESIAS:

Don't worry.—Now, let's have fun.

MYRRHINE:

No! Stop it! I said no!
—Although, of course,
I *do* love you.

KINESIAS:

I know you do. Darling Myrrhinê:
come, shall we?

MYRRHINE:

Are you out of your mind? In front of the child?

KINESIAS:

Take him home, Manês.

[*Exit* MANES *with* BABY

There. He's gone.

Come on!

There's nothing to stop us now.

MYRRHINE:

You devil! But where?

KINESIAS:

In Pan's cave. What could be snugger than that?

MYRRHINE:

But my purification before I go back to the Citadel?

KINESIAS:

Wash in the Klepsydra.

MYRRHINE:

And my oath?

KINESIAS:

Leave the oath to me.
After all, I'm the man.

MYRRHINE:

Well . . . if you say so.

I'll go find a bed.

KINESIAS:

Oh, bother a bed! The ground's good enough for me.

MYRRHINE:

No. You're a bad man, but you deserve something better
than dirt.

[*Exit* MYRRHINE

KINESIAS:

What a love she is! And how thoughtful!

[*Re-enter* MYRRHINE

MYRRHINE:

Here's your bed.
Now let me get my clothes off.

But, good horrors!

We haven't a mattress.
KINESIAS:
                    Oh, forget the mattress!
MYRRHINE:
                                              No.
Just lying on blankets? Too sordid.
KINESIAS:
                    Give me a kiss.
MYRRHINE:
    Just a second.
                                        [*Exit* MYRRHINE

KINESIAS:
                    I swear, I'll explode!
                                        [*Re-enter* MYRRHINE

MYRRHINE:
                              Here's your mattress.
    I'll just take my dress off.
                              But look—
    where's our pillow?
KINESIAS:
                    I don't *need* a pillow!
MYRRHINE:
                                        Well, *I* do.
                                        [*Exit* MYRRHINE

KINESIAS:
    I don't suppose even Heraklês
    would stand for this!
                                        [*Re-enter* MYRRHINE

MYRRHINE:
                    There we are. Ups-a-daisy!
KINESIAS:
    So we are. Well, come to bed.
MYRRHINE:
                              But I wonder:
    is everything ready now?
KINESIAS:
                              I can swear to that. Come, darling!
MYRRHINE:
    Just getting out of my girdle.
                              But remember, now,
    what you promised about the treaty.

KINESIAS:

Yes, yes, yes!

MYRRHINE:
But no coverlet!

KINESIAS:

Damn it, I'll be
your coverlet!

MYRRHINE:

Be right back.

[*Exit* MYRRHINE

KINESIAS:

This girl and her coverlets
will be the death of me.

[*Re-enter* MYRRHINE

MYRRHINE:

Here we are. Up you go!

KINESIAS:
Up? I've been up for ages.

MYRRHINE:

Some perfume?

KINESIAS:
No, by Apollo!

MYRRHINE:

Yes, by Aphroditê!
I don't care whether you want it or not.

[*Exit* MYRRHINE

KINESIAS:
For love's sake, hurry!

[*Re-enter* MYRRHINE

MYRRHINE:
Here, in your hand. Rub it right in.

KINESIAS:

Never cared for perfume.
And this is particularly strong. Still, here goes.

MYRRHINE:
What a nitwit I am! I brought you the Rhodian bottle.

KINESIAS:
Forget it.

MYRRHINE:

No trouble at all. You just wait here.

[*Exit* MYRRHINE

KINESIAS:

  God damn the man who invented perfume!

                       [*Re-enter* MYRRHINE

MYRRHINE:

  At last! The right bottle!

KINESIAS:

                I've got the rightest

  bottle of all, and it's right here waiting for you.

  Darling, forget everything else. Do come to bed.

MYRRHINE:

  Just let me get my shoes off.

                    —And, by the way,

  you'll vote for the treaty?

KINESIAS:

            I'll think about it.

                [MYRRHINE *runs away*

  There! That's done it! The damned woman,

  she gets me all bothered, she half kills me,

  and off she runs! What'll I do? Where

  can I get laid?

           —And you, little prodding pal,

  who's going to take care of *you*? No, you and I

  had better get down to old Foxdog's Nursing Clinic.

CHORUS[m]:

      Alas for the woes of man, alas

        Specifically for you.

      She's brought you to a pretty pass:

        What are you going to do?

      Split, heart! Sag, flesh! Proud spirit, crack!

      Myrrhinê's got you on your back.

KINESIAS:

      The agony, the protraction!

KORYPHAIOS[m]:

                  Friend,

      What woman's worth a damn?

      They bitch us all, world without end.

KINESIAS:

      Yet they're so damned sweet, man!

KORYPHAIOS^m:

      Calamitous, that's what I say.
      You should have learned that much today.

CHORUS^m:

      O blessed Zeus, roll womankind
        Up into one great ball;
      Blast them aloft on a high wind,
        And once there, let them fall.
      Down, down they'll come, the pretty dears,
      And split themselves on our thick spears.

                              [*Exit* KINESIAS

 SCENE IV

                        [*Enter a* SPARTAN HERALD

HERALD:

    Gentlemen, Ah beg you will be so kind
    as to direct me to the Central Committee.
    Ah have a communication.

                      [*Re-enter* COMMISSIONER

COMMISSIONER:

                  Are you a man,
    or a fertility symbol?

HERALD:

              Ah refuse to answer that question!
    Ah'm a certified herald from Spahta, and Ah've come
    to talk about an ahmistice.

COMMISSIONER:

              Then why
    that spear under your cloak?

HERALD:

              Ah have no speah!

COMMISSIONER:

    You don't walk naturally, with your tunic
    poked out so. You have a tumor, maybe,
    or a hernia?

HERALD:

        You lost yo' mahnd, man?

COMMISSIONER:

Well,
something's up, I can see that. And I don't like it.

HERALD:

Colonel, Ah resent this.

COMMISSIONER:

So I see. But what *is* it?

HERALD:

A staff
with a message from Spahta.

COMMISSIONER:

Oh. I know about those staffs.
Well, then, man, speak out: How are things in Sparta?

HERALD:

Hahd, Colonel, hahd! We're at a standstill.
Cain't seem to think of anything but women.

COMMISSIONER:

How curious! Tell me, do you Spartans think
that maybe Pan's to blame?

HERALD:

Pan? No. Lampitô and her little naked friends.
They won't let a man come nigh them.

COMMISSIONER:

How are you handling it?

HERALD:

Losing our mahnds,
if y' want to know, and walking around hunched over
lahk men carrying candles in a gale.
The women have swohn they'll have nothing to do with
us
until we get a treaty.

COMMISSIONER:

Yes. I know.
It's a general uprising, sir, in all parts of Greece.
But as for the answer—
Sir: go back to Sparta
and have them send us your Armistice Commission.
I'll arrange things in Athens.
And I may say
that my standing is good enough to make them listen.

HERALD:

A man after mah own haht! Seh, Ah thank you.

[*Exit* HERALD

🎗 CHORAL EPISODE

CHORUS^m:

        Oh these women! Where will you find [STROPHE
        A slavering beast that's more unkind?
          Where a hotter fire?
        Give me a panther, any day.
        He's not so merciless as they,
          And panthers don't conspire.

CHORUS^w:

        We may be hard, you silly old ass, [ANTISTROPHE
        But who brought you to this stupid pass?
          You're the ones to blame.
        Fighting with us, your oldest friends,
        Simply to serve your selfish ends—
          Really, you have no shame!

KORYPHAIOS^m:

No, I'm through with women for ever.

KORYPHAIOS^w:

                      If you say so.
Still, you might put some clothes on. You look too absurd
standing around naked. Come, get into this cloak.

KORYPHAIOS^m:

Thank you; you're right. I merely took it off
because I was in such a temper.

KORYPHAIOS^w:

                  That's much better.
Now you resemble a man again.
                  Why have you been so horrid?
And look: there's some sort of insect in your eye.
Shall I take it out?

KORYPHAIOS^m:

           An insect, is it? So that's
what's been bothering me. Lord, yes: take it out!

KORYPHAIOS^w:
You might be more polite.
　　　　　　　　—But, heavens!
What an enormous mosquito!

KORYPHAIOS^m:
　　　　　　　　You've saved my life.
That mosquito was drilling an artesian well
in my left eye.

KORYPHAIOS^w:
　　　　Let me wipe
those tears away.—And now: one little kiss?

KORYPHAIOS^m:
No, no kisses.

KORYPHAIOS^w:
　　　　You're so difficult.

KORYPHAIOS^m:
You impossible women! How you do get around us!
The poet was right: Can't live with you, or without you.
But let's be friends.
And to celebrate, you might join us in an Ode.

CHORUS^m and w:
　　　Let it never be said　　　　[STROPHE 1
　　　That my tongue is malicious:
　　　Both by word and by deed
I would set an example that's noble and gracious.
　　　We've had sorrow and care
　　　Till we're sick of the tune.
　　　Is there anyone here
　　　Who would like a small loan?
　　　My purse is crammed,
　　　As you'll soon find;
And you needn't pay me back if the Peace gets signed.

　　　I've invited to lunch　　　　[STROPHE 2
　　　Some Karystian rips—
　　　An esurient bunch,
But I've ordered a menu to water their lips.
　　　I can still make soup
　　　And slaughter a pig.
　　　You're all coming, I hope?

But a bath first, I beg!
                Walk right up
                As though you owned the place,
And you'll get the front door slammed to in your face.

🎐 SCENE V

[*Enter* SPARTAN AMBASSADOR, *with entourage*

KORYPHAIOS[m]:
    The Commission has arrived from Sparta.
                                                How oddly
    they're walking!
                Gentlemen, welcome to Athens!
    How is life in Lakonia?
AMBASSADOR:
                                Need we discuss that?
    Simply use your eyes.
CHORUS[m]:
                                The poor man's right:
                                What a sight!

AMBASSADOR:
                                                Words fail me.
    But come, gentlemen, call in your Commissioners,
    and let's get down to a Peace.
CHORAGOS[m]:
                                The state we're in! Can't bear
    a stitch below the waist. It's a kind of pelvic
    paralysis.
COMMISSIONER:
                Won't somebody call Lysistrata? —Gentlemen,
    we're no better off than you.
AMBASSADOR:
                                So I see.
A SPARTAN:
    Seh, do y'all feel a certain strain
    early in the morning?
AN ATHENIAN:
                                I do, sir. It's worse than a strain.

A few more days, and there's nothing for us but Kleisthenês,
that broken blossom.

CHORAGOS^m:

But you'd better get dressed again.
You know these people going around Athens with chisels,
looking for statues of Hermês.

ATHENIAN:

Sir, you are right.

SPARTAN:

He certainly is! Ah'll put mah own clothes back on.

[*Enter* ATHENIAN COMMISSIONERS

COMMISSIONER:

Gentlemen from Sparta, welcome. This
is a sorry business.

SPARTAN: [*To one of his own group:*

Colonel, we got dressed just in time. Ah sweah,
if they'd seen us the way we were, there'd have been a
new wah
between the states.

COMMISSIONER:

Shall we call the meeting to order?

Now, Lakonians,
what's your proposal?

AMBASSADOR:

We propose to consider peace.

COMMISSIONER:

Good. That's on our minds, too.

—Summon Lysistrata.
We'll never get anywhere without her.

AMBASSADOR:

Lysistrata?
Summon Lysis-*any*body! Only, summon!

KORYPHAIOS^m:

No need to summon:
here she is, herself.

[*Enter* LYSISTRATA

COMMISSIONER:

Lysistrata! Lion of women!
This is your hour to be

hard and yielding, outspoken and shy, austere and
gentle. You see here
the best brains of Hellas (confused, I admit,
by your devious charming) met as one man
to turn the future over to you.

LYSISTRATA:

                  That's fair enough,
unless you men take it into your heads
to turn to each other instead of to us. But I'd know
soon enough if you did.

                —Where is Reconciliation?
Go, some of you: bring her here.

                     [Exeunt two women
                And now, women,
lead the Spartan delegates to me: not roughly
or insultingly, as our men handle them, but gently,
politely, as ladies should. Take them by the hand,
or by anything else if they won't give you their hands.

              [The SPARTANS *are escorted over*
There. —The Athenians next, by any convenient handle.
              [The ATHENIANS *are escorted*
Stand there, please. —Now, all of you, listen to me.
    [During the following speech the two women
    re-enter, carrying an enormous statue of a naked
    girl; this is RECONCILIATION.
I'm only a woman, I know; but I've a mind,
and, I think, not a bad one: I owe it to my father
and to listening to the local politicians.
So much for that.

           Now, gentlemen,
since I have you here, I intend to give you a scolding.
We are all Greeks.
Must I remind you of Thermopylai, of Olympia,
of Delphoi? names deep in all our hearts?
Are they not a common heritage?

                 Yet you men
go raiding through the country from both sides,
Greek killing Greek, storming down Greek cities—
and all the time the Barbarian across the sea
is waiting for his chance!

            —That's my first point.

AN ATHENIAN:
  Lord! I can hardly contain myself.
LYSISTRATA:
                                    As for you Spartans:
  Was it so long ago that Perikleidês
  came here to beg our help? I can see him still,
  his grey face, his sombre gown. And what did he want?
  An army from Athens. All Messênê
  was hot at your heels, and the sea-god splitting your land.
  Well, Kimôn and his men,
  four thousand strong, marched out and saved all Sparta.
  And what thanks do we get? You come back to murder
    us.
AN ATHENIAN:
  They're aggressors, Lysistrata!
A SPARTAN:
                                  Ah admit it.
  When Ah look at those laigs, Ah sweah Ah'll aggress
    mahself!
LYSISTRATA:
  And you, Athenians: do you think you're blameless?
  Remember that bad time when we were helpless,
  and an army came from Sparta,
  and that was the end of the Thessalian menace,
  the end of Hippias and his allies.
                                    And that was Sparta,
  and only Sparta; but for Sparta, we'd be
  cringing slaves today, not free Athenians.
              [*From this point, the male responses are less to*
              LYSISTRATA *than to the statue*
A SPARTAN:
  A well shaped speech.
AN ATHENIAN:
                        Certainly it has its points.
LYSISTRATA:
  Why are we fighting each other? With all this history
  of favors given and taken, what stands in the way
  of making peace?
AMBASSADOR:
                    Spahta is ready, ma'am,
  so long as we get that place back.

LYSISTRATA:

What place, man?

AMBASSADOR:

Ah refer to Pylos.

COMMISSIONER:

Not a chance, by God!

LYSISTRATA:

Give it to them, friend.

COMMISSIONER:

But—what shall we have to bargain with?

LYSISTRATA:

Demand something in exchange.

COMMISSIONER:

Good idea. —Well, then:
Cockeville first, and the Happy Hills, and the country
between the Legs of Mégara.

AMBASSADOR:

Mah government objects.

LYSISTRATA:

Over-ruled. Why fuss about a pair of legs?
                    [General assent. The statue is removed.

AN ATHENIAN:

I want to get out of these clothes and start my plowing.

A SPARTAN:

Ah'll fertilize mahn first, by the Heavenly Twins!

LYSISTRATA:

And so you shall,
once you've made peace. If you are serious,
go, both of you, and talk with your allies.

COMMISSIONER:

Too much talk already. No, we'll stand together.
We've only one end in view. All that we want
is our women; and I speak for our allies.

AMBASSADOR:

Mah government concurs.

AN ATHENIAN:

So does Karystos.

LYSISTRATA:

Good. —But before you come inside
to join your wives at supper, you must perform

the usual lustration. Then we'll open
our baskets for you, and all that we have is yours.
But you must promise upright good behavior
from this day on. Then each man home with his woman!

AN ATHENIAN:

Let's get it over with.

A SPARTAN:

                Lead on. Ah follow.

AN ATHENIAN:

Quick as a cat can wink!

                [Exeunt all but the CHORUSES

CHORUS^W:

          Embroideries ánd   [ANTISTROPHE 1
          Twinkling ornaments ánd
          Pretty dresses—I hand
Them all over to you, and with never a qualm.
          They'll be nice for your daughters
          On festival days
          When the girls bring the Goddess
          The ritual prize.
               Come in, one and all:
               Take what you will.
I've nothing here so tightly corked that you can't make
   it spill.

          You may search my house,   [ANTISTROPHE 2
          But you'll not find
          The least thing of use,
Unless your two eyes are keener than mine.
          Your numberless brats
          Are half starved? and your slaves?
          Courage, grandpa! I've lots
          Of grain left, and big loaves.
               I'll fill your guts,
               I'll go the whole hog;
But if you come too close to me, remember: 'ware the
   dog!

                [Exeunt CHORUSES

🥀 ÉXODOS

> [*A* DRUNKEN CITIZEN *enters, approaches the gate,
> and is halted by a sentry*

CITIZEN:
Open. The. Door.
SENTRY:
                        Now, friend, just shove along!
—So you want to sit down. If it weren't such an old joke,
I'd tickle your tail with this torch. Just the sort of gag
this audience appreciates.
CITIZEN:
                      I. Stay. Right. Here.

SENTRY:
Get away from there, or I'll scalp you! The gentlemen
    from Sparta
are just coming back from dinner.
> [*Exit* CITIZEN; *the general company re-enters;
> the two* CHORUSES *now represent* SPARTANS *and*
> ATHENIANS.

A SPARTAN:
                         Ah must say,
Ah never tasted better grub.
AN ATHENIAN:
                      And those Lakonians!
They're gentlemen, by the Lord! Just goes to show,
a drink to the wise is sufficient.
COMMISSIONER:
                      And why not?
A sober man's an ass.
Men of Athens, mark my words: the only efficient
Ambassador's a drunk Ambassador. Is that clear?
Look: we go to Sparta,
and when we get there we're dead sober. The result?
Everyone cackling at everyone else. They make speeches;
and even if we understand, we get it all wrong
when we file our reports in Athens. But today—!
Everybody's happy. Couldn't tell the difference
between *Drink to Me Only* and
The Star-Spangled Athens.

What's a few lies,
washed down in good strong drink?
[*Re-enter the* DRUNKEN CITIZEN

SENTRY:

God almighty,

he's back again!
CITIZEN:

I. Resume. My. Place.
A SPARTAN: [*To an* ATHENIAN
Ah beg yo', seh,
take yo' instrument in yo' hand and play for us.
Ah'm told
yo' understand the in*tric*acies of the floot?
Ah'd lahk to execute a song and dance
in honor of Athens,
and, of cohse, of Spahta.

CITIZEN:
Toot. On. Your. Flute.

[*The following song is a solo—an aria—accompanied by the flute. The* CHORUS OF SPARTANS *begins a slow dance.*

A SPARTAN:
O Memory,
Let the Muse speak once more
In my young voice. Sing glory.
Sing Artemision's shore,
Where Athens fluttered the Persians. *Alalai*,
Sing glory, that great
Victory! Sing also
Our Leonidas and his men,
Those wild boars, sweat and blood
Down in a red drench. Then, then
The barbarians broke, though they had stood
Numberless as the sands before!

O Artemis,
Virgin Goddess, whose darts
Flash in our forests: approve
This pact of peace and join our hearts,

From this day on, in love.
Huntress, descend!

LYSISTRATA:

All that will come in time.
                    But now, Lakonians,
take home your wives. Athenians, take yours.
Each man be kind to his woman; and you, women,
be equally kind. Never again, pray God,
shall we lose our way in such madness.

KORYPHAIOS[a]:

                              And now
let's dance our joy.
                    [*From this point the dance becomes general*

CHORUS[a]:

Dance, you Graces
                    Artemis, dance
Dance, Phoibos, Lord of dancing
                              Dance,
In a scurry of Maenads, Lord Dionysos
                    Dance, Zeus Thunderer
          Dance, Lady Hêra
Queen of the Sky
                    Dance, dance, all you gods
Dance witness everlasting of our pact
Evohí Evohé
Dance for the dearest
                    the Bringer of Peace
Deathless Aphroditê!

COMMISSIONER:

Now let us have another song from Sparta.

CHORUS[B]:

          From Taÿgetos, from Taÿgetos,
          Lakonian Muse, come down.
          Sing to the Lord Apollo
          Who rules Amyklai Town.

Sing Athêna of the House of Brass!

Sing Lêda's Twins, that chivalry
    Resplendent on the shore
Of our Eurôtas; sing the girls
    That dance along before:

Sparkling in dust their gleaming feet,
    Their hair a Bacchant fire,
And Lêda's daughter, thyrsos raised,
    Leads their triumphant choir.

CHORUSES a and a:
    Evohé!
        Evohai!
            Evohé!
                We pass
        Dancing
            dancing
                to greet
    Athêna of the House of Brass.

NOTES

Page

9: *those heavenly eels*: See note on BOIOTIA.

11: *that dance of ahs*: Athenian girls were brought up in seclusion. In Sparta, however, girls were expected to participate in athletic exercises. The 'dance' referred to here is the strenuous *bibasis,* in which the executant must strike her buttocks with her heels.

11: *Lawdy*: She swears 'by the Two,' which, in Sparta, meant the Heavenly Twins, Kastor and Polydeukês. The Athenian 'by the Two' was reserved to women only, and referred to Demêter and Persephonê.

12: *that General*: His name was Eukratês, and Σ describes him as 'an Athenian general, for sale, a traitor, and a mercenary'.

13: *drink up the proceeds*: The Athenian women were frequently satirized as being heavy drinkers.—The joke here, such as it is, depends upon a rhetorical trope by which the expected conclusion of a sentence is twisted into an unexpected incongruity. Thus, one would have expected Myrrhinê to say that she would pawn her best dress and contribute the proceeds to the Cause.

14: *when he saw Helen's breast*: An allusion to Euripides' *Andromachê,* 627, *sqq;* where Menelaos, about to stab his faithless wife, is overcome by her beauty and drops his sword.

16: *Where's our Inner Guard?*: See note on SKYTHIANS.

16: *Why not a white horse?*: Obscure; Σ observes that 'the horse' is a schema of coitus, but he also remarks that the Amazons (see note on MIKON) were accustomed to sacrifice white horses. According to Herodotos, the Amazons, furious horsewomen, were noted for their white (we should say 'ash-blonde') hair.

20: *the sacred statuar-y*: The august statue of Athêna Polias, which fell from Heaven upon the Akropolis.

22: *Trito-born!*: Name for Athêna, who, according to some accounts, was born near Lake Tritonis, in Libya.

25: *troops for Sicily*: A reference to the elaborate Sicilian Expedition (415 B.C.), in which Athens suffered a calamitous defeat from which she never recovered. (See note on DEMO-STRATOS.)

31: *"War's / a man's affair"*: Quoted from *Iliad* VI:492; Hektor to Andromachê.

36: *I bore the vessels*: Annually, four girls of high birth, between the ages of seven and eleven, were appointed acolytes to Athêna in the Akropolis.

36: *I was pounding out the barley*: At the age of ten, an aristocratic girl was eligible to be chosen as Mill-maid; her duty was to grind the sacred grain for Athêna.

36: *Little Bear*: See note on BRAURON.

36: *the Holy Basket*: The highest distinction of all. According to Σ, the baskets containing objects sacred to Athêna were of gold.

37: *our Treasury*: A sum of money, originally contributed by Athens and her allies, intended to finance an extension of the sea-war against Persia. Since the failure of the Sicilian Expedition, the contributions of the allies had fallen off; and the fund itself was now being raided by Athenian politicians.

39: *Pan's cave*: A grotto on the north side of the Akropolis, beneath the walls.

41: *the Snake*: This divine Snake was the Guardian of the Temple, the peculiar Safeguard of the Akropolis. He never appeared; but each month a succulent cake was set out for him, and it always vanished overnight.

41: *those horrible owls*: The Owl was sacred to Athêna.

46: *Oh, this mother business!*: A parody of Euripides, *Iph. Aul.* 917.

57: *looking for statues*: The statues were the Hermai, stone posts set up in various parts of Athens. Just before the sailing of the Sicilian Expedition, a group of anonymous vandals mutilated these statues with chisels. This and the women's Adonis-dirge (see note on ADONIS) were considered unhappy auguries.

57: *Summon Lysis-anybody!*: He actually says 'Lysistratos,' grasping at random for a name. Lysistrata's name means Dissolver of Armies.

64: *Athêna of the House of Brass*: This famous temple stood on the Akropolis of Sparta.

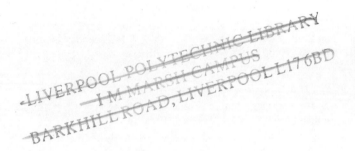